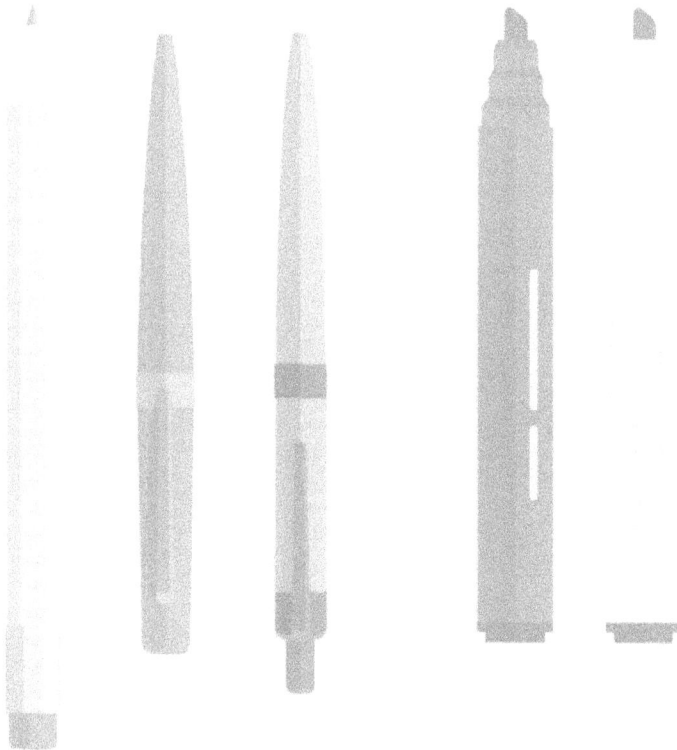

SCRIPTURIENT BOOKS

PAPER HEARTS WORKBOOK
Copyright © 2017 by Beth Revis

www.bethrevis.com

First paperback edition: 2017

The author is available for instructional workshops for groups or individuals. Contact via her website for more information.

PAPER HEARTS
Workbook

Beth Revis

CONTENTS

Foreword

Focusing on Goals

Iceberg Knowledge

Developing Voice

Developing Story

Structure & Plotting

Next Steps

For additional online resources,
visit http://bethrevis.com/paperhearts

FOREWORD

YOU DON'T NEED THIS BOOK.

I mean, I do hope this workbook helps you, not only in brainstorming your own book, but also in developing practices that help you write for a career in publication. I hope it helps you organize your ideas, work through problems, and learn new things about your plot and characters.

But you don't need it.

If you want to do all those things—brainstorm, organize, and more—you can do it on your own. Blank paper will work just fine. Find your focus and narrow in on your ideas.

But for some, the blank page is a bit intimidating.

That's what this workbook is for: Helping to make the blank page less intimidating and giving you a foundation to uncover your own story. My goal is for you to move from idea to completed novel or from a completed draft to a polished revision.

Every activity in this book is designed to be used by people in any stage of their novel. Whether you're planning, drafting, or revising, each activity can help you—it just depends on where you find yourself stuck.

Just as there is no one right way to write, there's no one right way to work on the activities in this book. Some will find it helpful to start with nothing but an idea and plan everything right here. Some will find it helpful to jump around to specific activities for specific problems they're having. Some won't want to use this workbook until they finish their first draft, choosing to use the activities to help revise.

A few of the activities are designed to be completed with others. Writing is often lonely, but revising rarely is; critique partners, editors, and beta readers can bring your work to the next level, so a few of the activities here are designed with them in mind.

And finally, you'll find some activities here lend themselves to what happens after you finish the novel. By the time you complete this workbook, you'll not only have your novel, but also a tagline and pitch paragraph for a query letter for agents or a blurb if you plan to self publish.

FOCUSING ON GOALS

THIS SECTION IS ARGUABLY THE most important of the entire workbook. A clear sense of purpose and goals is often the difference between a hobbyist and a professional. These goals extend past the immediate—to finish a book—and into the long-term realities of developing habits that will enable you to better be a professional writer.

Often, we writers are dreamers who dream big. And our goals reflect that. We want to hit the *NY Times* bestseller's list, or make a million dollars, or quit our day job in a blaze of glory. And those goals are important—but they're not something we can control. So feel free to list the dreams, but focus also on what you can do and how you can make those things happen.

I hope you look back to this section in the future—see what goals you've accomplished, and which ones have shifted. **And remember: There's nothing wrong with changing your goals over time; just make sure you always strive toward *something*.**

Also in this section is a schedule that focuses not so much on daily goals, but overall deadlines. Some people thrive by writing every day, but others don't. The important thing isn't that you write every day, but that you finish your goals in a timeframe that works best for you. Your schedule can be flexible—feel free to adjust your schedule as you need to. Life happens. Creativity happens—meaning you have to rewrite the novel, or get a second round of critiques. These things take time...just make sure you don't waste time and always keep an eye on the end goal.

And finally, the last activities in this section conclude with a narrowed focus on your specific book. You may not be able to complete your stats or details of the pitch at the start—but fill it in as you go, so that by the time you finish the novel, you also have a grounding for how to focus on revisions and then sell the book.

CHECKLIST
What do you need to tell a story?

❑ An idea

But it also helps to have:

❑ A strong work ethic

❑ Determination to see it through to completion

❑ Time set aside to focus on work

❑ Knowledge that the first draft will not be good enough

❑ Acceptance that there is both joy in creation and work in completion

❑ A little luck

GOALS

What is the biggest goal that you can achieve independent of luck or help from others?	
What is your dream goal for this project— something that's not directly in your control but that you wish would happen?	
What, to you, will mean that this project is successful?	
What is the most important habit you need to develop to make this project a success?	

FOCUSED DEVELOPMENT

Title	
Genre	
Target Audience	
Target Word Count	

What is the original idea for your story? What's your goal in telling this story?

_____

_____

_____

_____

_____

What books, movies, art, events, etc. originally inspired this story?

_____

_____

_____

_____

_____

What published books explore similar ideas or themes?

_____

_____

_____

_____

_____

How will your book be different from the ones already published?

_____

_____

_____

_____

_____

PERSONAL SCHEDULE

Start Date	
Goal Completion Date	
DEADLINES	
Complete Planning	
Write Opening Scene	
Write 25k Words	
Write First Half of Novel	
Complete First Draft of Novel	
Finish Reading & Self Edits (Don't forget to take time to gain distance!)	
Receive Feedback from Readers	
Complete Revisions Based on Readers' Feedback	
For traditional publication: Submit to agents *For self publication:* Submit to hired editor	
I will start working on my next book by this date:	

Finished!

INSPIRATION TRIANGLE

Most stories start with a simple question: *What if?* But to develop that question into a story, you need to ask why such a situation would happen in the first place, how it came came about, and who is involved in the story.

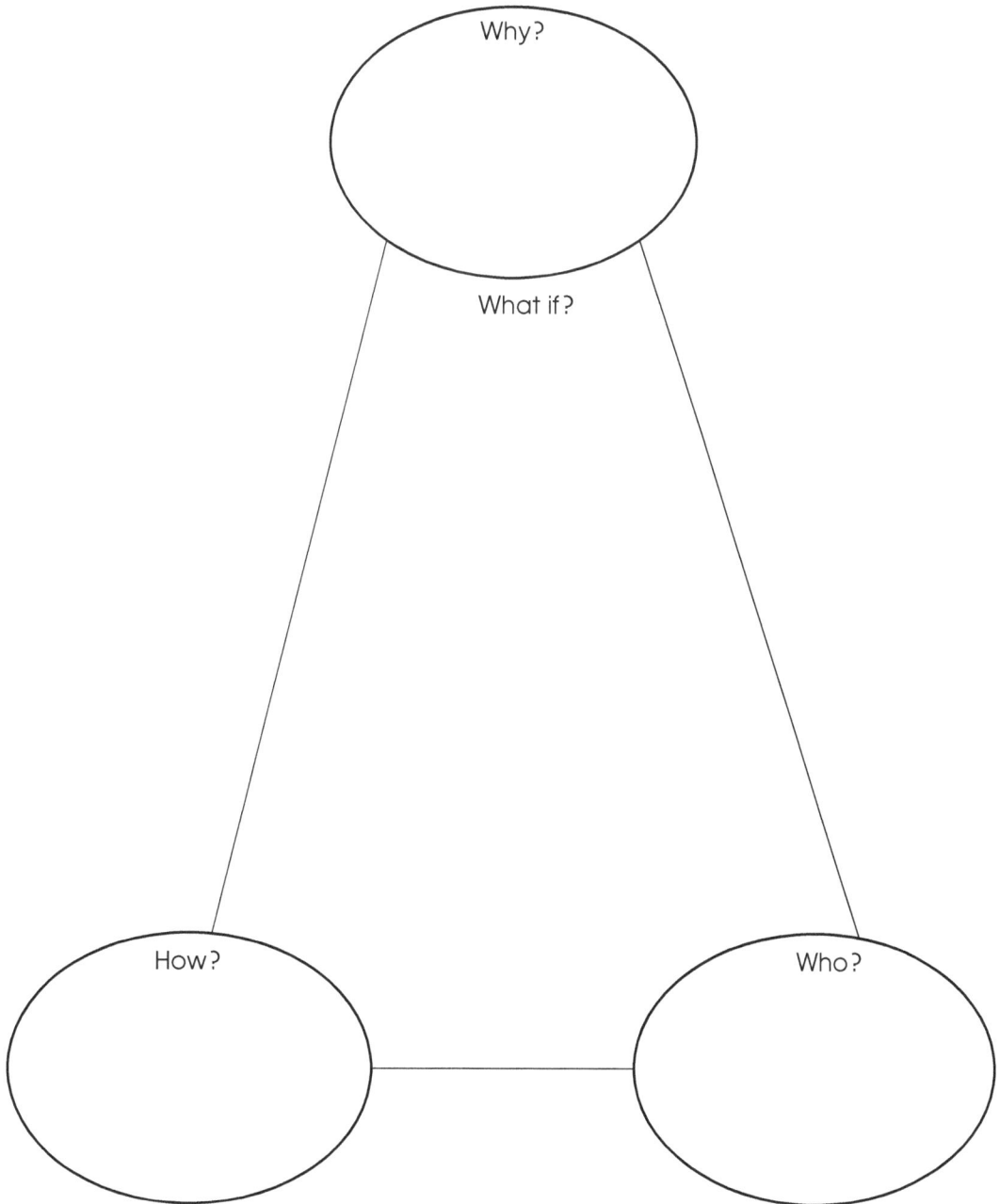

Why?

What if?

How?

Who?

HIGH CONCEPT: Examples

There's no new idea under the sun. But even if the idea isn't new, the story is. Showing how an idea is similar, such as by fitting into a specific genre or trope, and then quickly and easily showing how they are unique is a key selling point in high concept stories. Alternatively, sometimes the unique angle lies in blending pre-existing tropes and genres. Regardless, the twist is often what sets the work apart.

Examples

GENRE OR TROPE	SPECIFIC DETAILS	TWIST	TITLE
Dystopian	People fight to the death in an arena	The people are children	*The Hunger Games*
Vampires	A subset of vampires are actually good	It's a love story	*Twilight*
Futuristic	Only the main character can alter others' memories	Someone's altered her memory	*The Body Electric*
GENRE/TROPE 1	**GENRE/TROPE 2**	**TWIST**	**TITLE**
Chosen One	Boarding School	Wizards	*Harry Potter*
Chosen One	Science Fiction	Space Wizards	*Star Wars*
Space Sci Fi	Murder Mystery	Romance	*Across the Universe*

HIGH CONCEPT: Application

"Excellence is to do a common thing in an uncommon way."
–Booker T Washington

Think about how your book is common, using genres or tropes, and then think of how it stands out. Remember, simple is better here—be as succinct as possible!

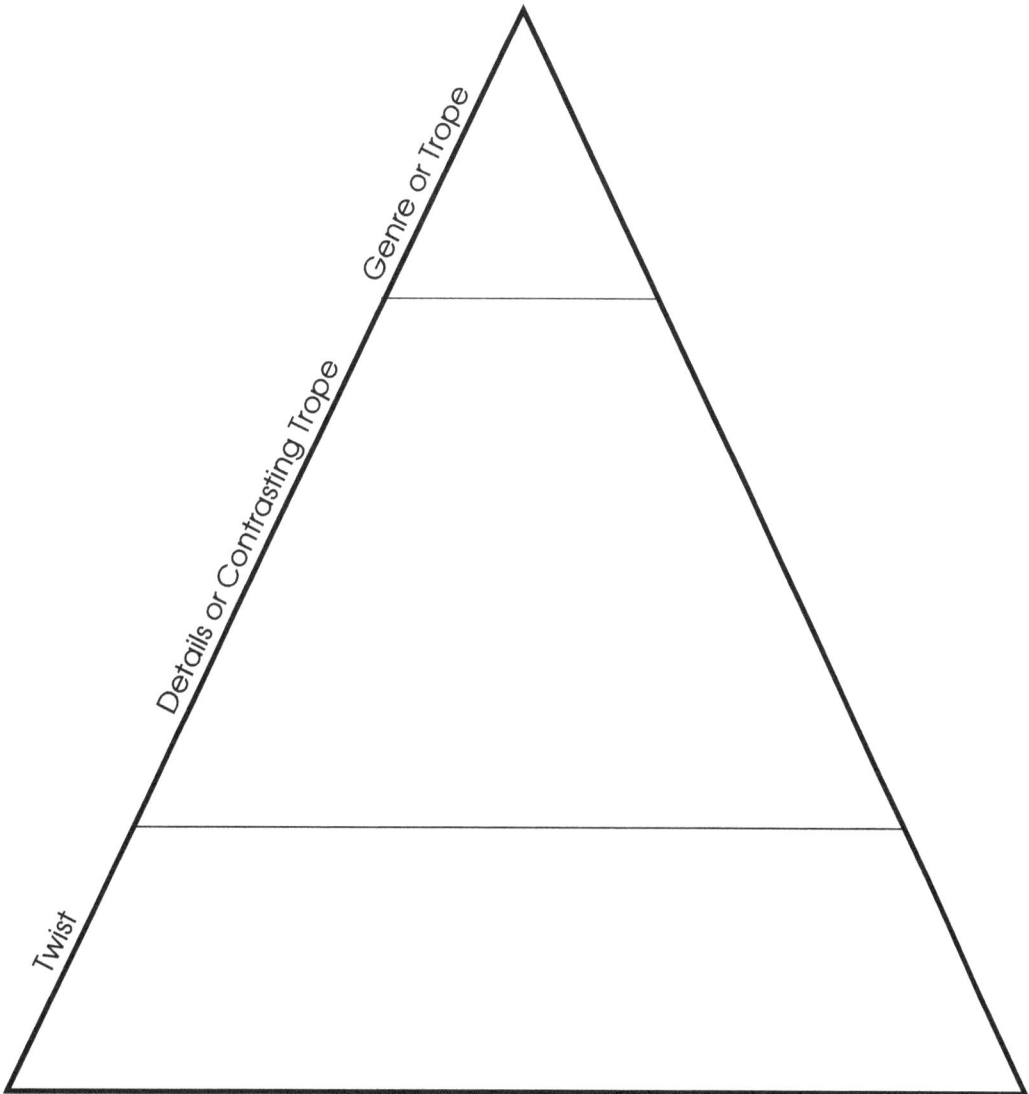

Genre or Trope

Details or Contrasting Trope

Twist

DEVELOPING PITCH: Tips

It often helps to know your pitch even before you write your book; it keeps you focused on the story you want to tell without getting sidetracked. Knowing how you want to pitch your book helps you after you finish as well.

Later in this workbook, we focus on developing a pitch that can be used professionally. For now, however, keep it casual and just for you. On the following pages, sum up your story in a sentence, a paragraph, and a page. But *don't* stress about it. It doesn't have to be pretty. I find it helps me to pretend I'm telling the details of the story to someone who's never heard of it before—it becomes like a conversation with an interested friend. **But don't make this too polished.** There is value in just talking about your story without thinking of how you have to sell it.

Tips:

- One-Sentence Pitch:
    - Keep it as simple as possible.
    - Focus on the twist of your story—what makes it unique?
    - It may be easier to write it as a comparison: "X meets Y."
    - Don't cram as much as you can into it. It's called a one-sentence pitch because it should be short. In fact, two small sentences is better than one over-long sentence.
- Pitch Paragraph:
    - Focus on the main characters and the main plots only.
    - Although it's called a "paragraph," feel free to break it up stylistically into shorter paragraphs.
    - Tease the story, but don't give away the end. Instead, give the final conflict without the solution.
- One-Page Synopsis:
    - Tone and voice are important, but it's more important to tell the whole story. Err on the side of easy-to-understand.
    - Give the whole plot, including the ending of the book.
    - Try to show how lessons learned in the beginning are relevant to the end of the story.
    - Succinctly mention any major subplots.
- **Throughout this activity, remember: this is for *you*, no one else. Tell yourself your story in a succinct way.** Blank pages are included at the end of this activity for you to brainstorm. You may find it easier to think through this if you split the story up into acts.

DEVELOPING PITCH:
Application

Complete these as you develop your story. Don't be afraid to rewrite them if your story changes later. An extra page for notes is included, as well as a blank page for brainstorming.

REMEMBER: THIS IS JUST A ROUGH DRAFT. There are other sections in this workbook for perfecting your pitch for submission. Use this space to figure out your story and focus your ideas.

One Sentence Pitch

_____
_____
_____

Pitch Paragraph

_____
_____
_____
_____
_____
_____
_____
_____
_____
_____
_____
_____
_____
_____
_____
_____
_____

One Page Summary

_____

_____

_____

_____

_____

_____

_____

_____

_____

_____

_____

_____

_____

_____

_____

_____

_____

_____

_____

_____

_____

_____

_____

_____

_____

_____

_____

_____

_____

_____

_____

_____

_____

_____

Notes & Changes

ACCOUNTABILITY

As you write, you may find it useful to check in with a writer buddy to make sure you keep to your schedule. Develop a set of goals with a partner, and check in with them to make sure you actually stick to your schedule.

Goal to Meet	Check-In Date	Goal Met? (Circle one)
		Yes No
		Yes No
		Yes No
		Yes No
		Yes No
		Yes No
		Yes No
		Yes No

JOURNAL

Why am I the person to tell this story?

Take a moment to reflect on your idea and what you want to do with your book. What makes you the person to tell this story in this way? What is your personal connection to the story or the characters? Why are you the only person who could write this story?

_____

_____

_____

_____

_____

_____

_____

_____

_____

_____

_____

_____

_____

_____

_____

_____

_____

_____

_____

_____

_____

_____

_____

_____

_____

_____

_____

_____

END SECTION NOTES

ICEBERG KNOWLEDGE

AS THE WRITER, NO ONE KNOWS MORE about your story than you. What a reader sees is could only be ten percent of the work you actually put into writing the book. Similarly, icebergs hide ninety percent of their mass underwater, with only ten percent remaining visible. I call the parts of the story that are never seen by the reader "iceberg knowledge"—the hidden work.

For some, this feels like a waste. You invest time and energy into developing detailed backgrounds for your characters and world, and the reader never sees any of it.

Often, trimming down a story is more difficult than adding additional details. And this section of the workbook is entirely about getting to know those details that you will not ever put in your final manuscript.

This is not wasted energy, though! The writer *should* know more about the story than what ends up on the page. Knowing these details will help you write a more nuanced story and will help you trust yourself as you create purposeful characterizations and details within your plot and world.

As you complete the activities in this section, keep in mind **almost none of the details here should be explicitly stated within your final manuscript.** While, for example, I ask you to list your character's fears, try not to ever state that your character has these fears. Instead, *show* the fears through the character's reactions within the story.

Much of iceberg knowledge deals directly with the problem of showing versus telling the reader the story, as well as learning to trust the reader. As you take these activities and apply them to your work, focus on trusting your reader to see beneath the surface.

UNDERSTANDING ICEBERG CHARACTERS

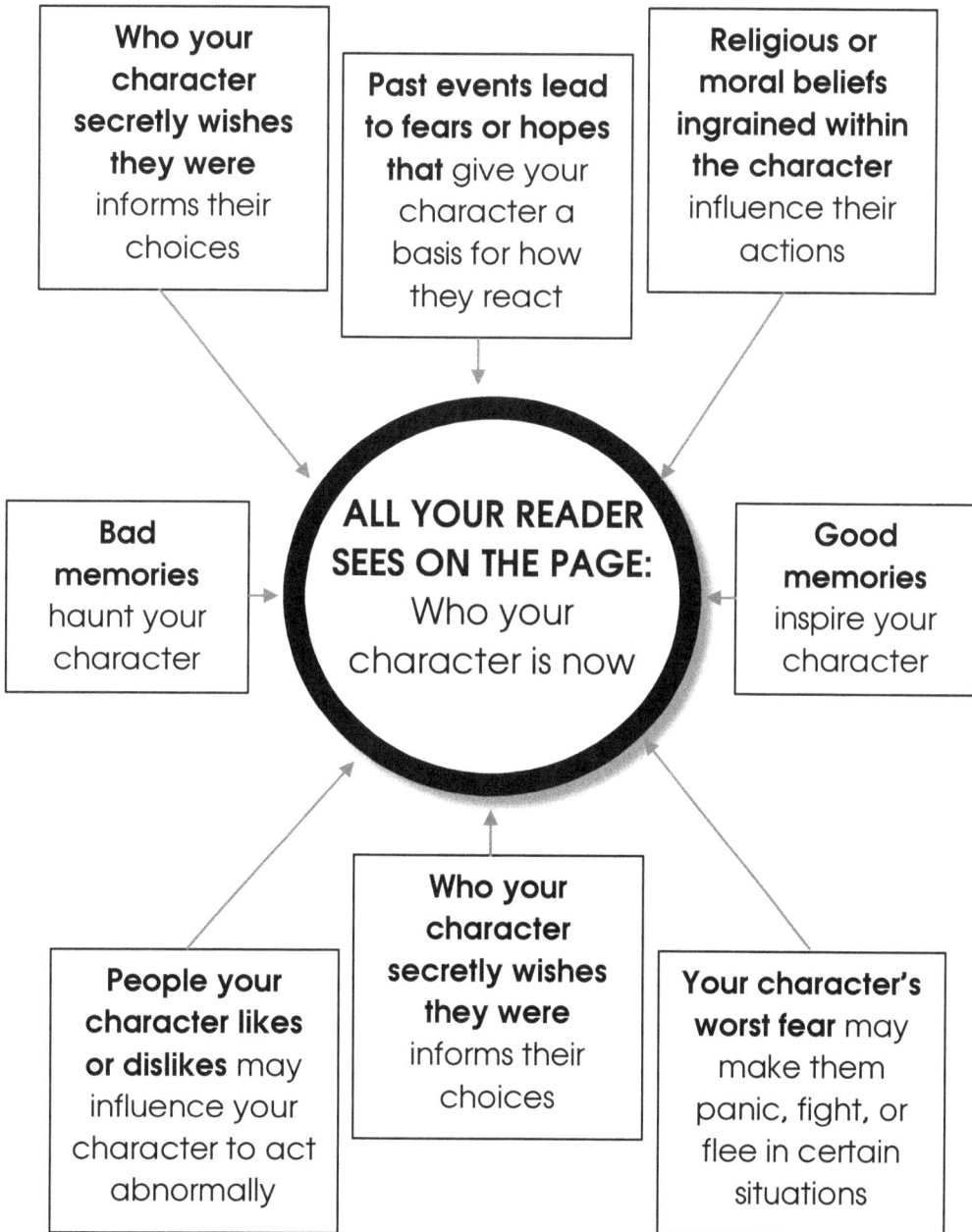

Who your character secretly wishes they were informs their choices

Past events lead to fears or hopes that give your character a basis for how they react

Religious or moral beliefs ingrained within the character influence their actions

Bad memories haunt your character

ALL YOUR READER SEES ON THE PAGE: Who your character is now

Good memories inspire your character

People your character likes or dislikes may influence your character to act abnormally

Who your character secretly wishes they were informs their choices

Your character's worst fear may make them panic, fight, or flee in certain situations

ICEBERG CHARACTERIZATION

Apply this concept to your main character. Consider key signature attitudes, actions, and/or traits that your character does within the story, and develop *why* the character acts or believes in this way. Dig into your character's psyche and past—*especially* the things not on the page.

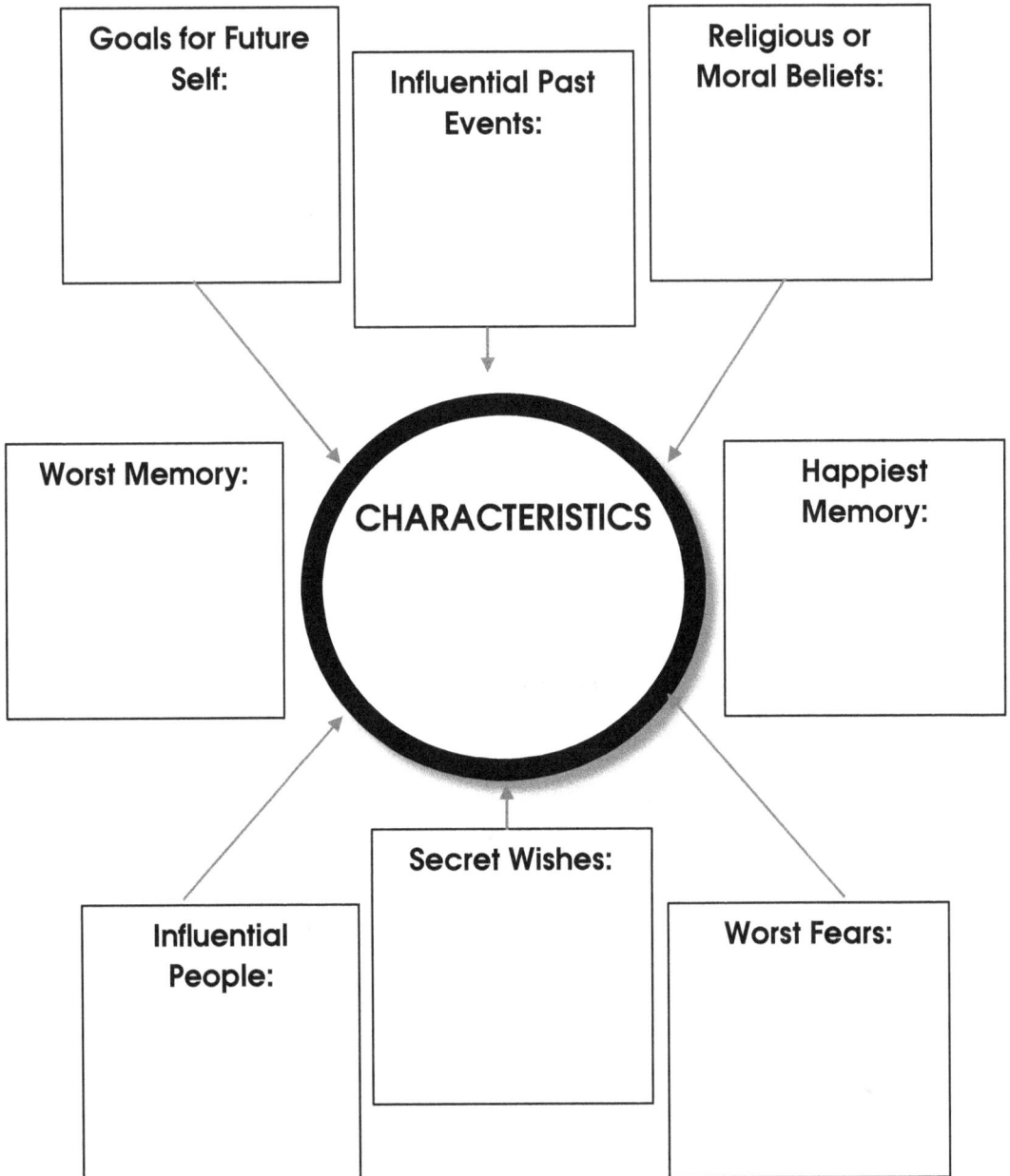

Goals for Future Self:

Influential Past Events:

Religious or Moral Beliefs:

Worst Memory:

CHARACTERISTICS

Happiest Memory:

Secret Wishes:

Influential People:

Worst Fears:

FEAR, PAIN, & IDENTITY

Fear and pain are among the most defining influencers of a character's identity, so honing in on them in more detail is important. Remember, the things you list do *not* have to be directly related to the story you're writing. Think of your characters as real people with real histories.

STEP ONE: PAIN	STEP TWO: FEAR
List a few events that happened in your character's past that caused the character pain	List fears that your character has, big or small. Try to connect them to past painful events.

STEP THREE: IDENTITY

Write a short scene where you *show* how your character is afraid of something without actually stating what that fear is. Think in terms of reactions and motivations for actions.

LIES & TRUTHS

In the beginning of the novel, it's common for a character to believe a core lie about him or herself. This lie is revealed to be untrue over the course of the novel. Often, the lie is that a character believes they aren't good enough, or worthy, or able to change. It can be simpler, such as a character who feels they are trapped. Explore this core lie.

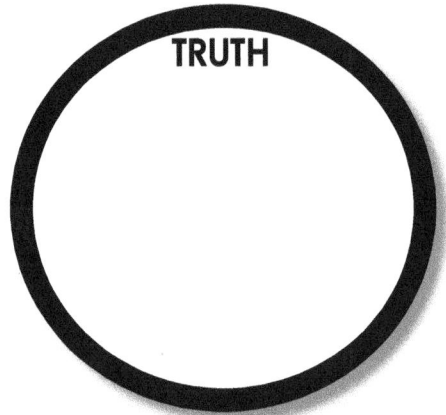

LIE

TRUTH

Why does the character believe this lie?	How does the character discover the truth?

EXPOSING SECRETS

Your character finds a bag of money on the street. The money came from a rich person who doesn't notice its loss, and no one knows your character has it. In other words, no one but your character knows where the money came from and keeping it would cause no harm to the original owner of the money. **Write a paragraph or brainstorm what your character would do in this situation.** Would your character keep it and use it selfishly? Return it, despite the owner not caring? Donate it to charity? **Expose who your character is by describing what they do.**

_____
_____
_____
_____
_____
_____
_____
_____
_____
_____
_____
_____
_____
_____
_____
_____
_____
_____
_____
_____
_____
_____
_____
_____
_____
_____
_____
_____

NAILING HIDDEN CHARACTERS

Show a partner your notes on the iceberg details of your character, with the exception of the "Exposing Secrets" activity. Without guiding your partner, have them write a paragraph here on what your character would do in the moral situation presented. Does it match what *you* expected your character to do? Compare the different interpretations.

PROMPT: The character finds a bag of money on the street. The money came from a rich person who doesn't notice its loss, and no one knows the character has it. In other words, no one but the character knows where the money came from, and keeping it would cause no harm to the original owner of the money. **What does the character do with the money?**

_____

_____

_____

_____

_____

_____

_____

_____

_____

_____

_____

_____

_____

_____

_____

_____

_____

_____

_____

_____

_____

_____

_____

JOURNAL

What is the beating heart of my story?

Often, writers have a deeper reason for why they write a particular story in a particular way. The meaning of the story—the *heart* of the story—is the uncompromising center of what they want to say.

What's your story's heart?

_____

_____

_____

_____

_____

_____

_____

_____

_____

_____

_____

_____

_____

_____

_____

_____

_____

_____

_____

_____

_____

_____

_____

_____

_____

_____

_____

_____

END SECTION NOTES

DEVELOPING VOICE

THERE IS NO NEW STORY UNDER THE SUN, so what sets *your* story apart isn't what you say, but how you say it. Developing a unique voice is often what makes or breaks a new novel.

The defining characteristic of voice lies in perspective. Showing your character's unique perspective through opinions, reactions, beliefs, and attitudes gives the reader the lens through which to view the story. Consider, for example, Shakespeare's *Hamlet.* Told from Hamlet's point of view, with his perspective of the story, results in a tale of unjust grabs for power foiled by a son's mission to avenge his father. Switch that perspective to Ophelia and you have a woman's life ruined by her lover's single-minded obsession with revenge. Changing the perspective changes the voice, and the voice is what makes the story unique and singular.

As you complete the activities in this section, keep in mind how vital perspective and point of view are to the way a story is told. Developing the voice trickles down to every other aspect of writing. A unique voice influences how a character is presented to the reader, how the character views the world they live in, and what choices the character makes to further the storyline and plot.

NEUTRAL LENS

Describe an object relevant to your story as simply as possible, using only facts. Be specific, but without any bias or opinions of your own.

OBJECT			
What does it look like?	What does it sound like? (Either by itself, or if dropped or tapped.)	What does it taste and/or smell like?	What does it feel like?

Creating a description based only on these facts would be specific and informative, but probably also boring. This is a neutral, unbiased description. Thinking instead of how your character would see the object—bringing with them their experiences, opinions, and attitudes—is what provides the character's lens of the story.

CHARACTER LENS

Describe an object as simply as possible, using only facts. Then describe this object from other characters' points of view. How do they see the object? Do they associate it with anything else? What do they want to do with it? **Remember:** Use more senses than just sight.

Object & Description:		
Character 1	**Character 2**	**Character 3**
Name:	Name:	Name:
How would each character view the object?		

KNOW YOUR CHARACTER

STEP ONE:
Use an index card to list the defining attributes of a character, including influential past events, beliefs, and the most important aspects that affect the character's view of the world. On the top of the card, write the character's name so it will be easier to return the card to the owner.

STEP TWO:
Swap index cards with a partner. This is often effective done in larger groups.

STEP THREE:
Select a random object in the room and allow all participants to inspect it.

STEP THREE:
Each person uses a new index card to describe an object from the point of view of the character described on the character card. List the character's name on top. *Note:* If the character is not from our world and/or if the object would be unknown to the character, pretend that the object is commonplace within the character's world for the purposes of this activity.

STEP FOUR:
Swap character cards again and repeat with other objects until each character card has a brief description written by all authors.

STEP FIVE:
Return the character card and all description cards to the original authors. Authors, inspect the descriptions and analyze what insights the descriptions with lenses give to characters.

WORLD BUILDING LENS

Make the world your characters live in dirty, rough, scratched and, well, *lived in*. We often touch on only the surface level details, the features that are immediately necessary for the story. Write a short scene here describing part of your world that shows evidence of wear or use—that shows the world has as much of a past as your characters do.

_____

_____

_____

_____

_____

_____

_____

_____

_____

_____

Put that scene in perspective. Is there any part of the description that can give your character insight? That could be a metaphor? That is parallel to or opposite from some aspect in your story? Make it significant to the story.

_____

_____

_____

_____

_____

_____

_____

_____

_____

_____

BONUS: "Chekhov's gun" is a common dramatic principle named for the advice Anton Chekhov wrote: "If in the first act you have hung a pistol on the wall, then in the following one it should be fired. Otherwise don't put it there." Can this somewhat obscure feature of the world be a clue to something larger within your plot as a whole? *Example:* A character notices a book with a worn cover, which reminds her of her mother's love for antiques. Later that book is revealed to hide a note from her mother.

TYING CHARACTER TO PLOT

Your characters' specific attitudes, beliefs, and opinions define what they do when they are presented with problems. The consequences of their actions as they tackle the problems often lead the character to change. Examine the ways these interact using one character and one problem.

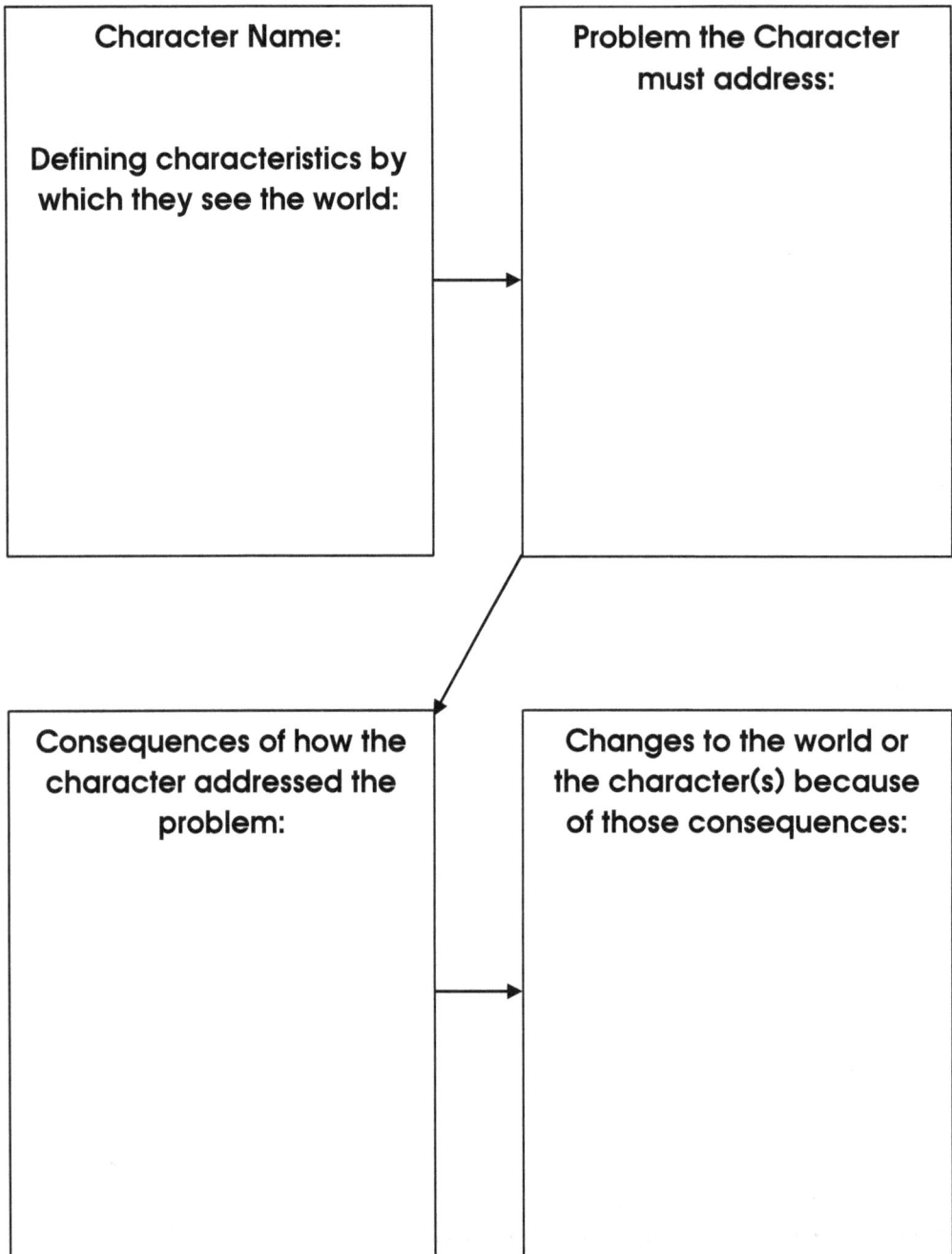

Character Name:

Defining characteristics by which they see the world:

Problem the Character must address:

Consequences of how the character addressed the problem:

Changes to the world or the character(s) because of those consequences:

JOURNAL

What is your lens within the story?

All writing is informed by our lived experiences. How has your own life influenced the way in which you see your characters and story?

_____

_____

_____

_____

_____

_____

_____

_____

_____

_____

_____

_____

_____

_____

_____

_____

_____

_____

_____

_____

_____

_____

_____

_____

_____

_____

_____

_____

_____

_____

END SECTION NOTES

_____
_____
_____
_____
_____
_____
_____
_____
_____
_____
_____
_____
_____
_____
_____
_____
_____
_____
_____
_____
_____
_____
_____
_____
_____
_____
_____
_____
_____

DEVELOPING STORY

THE RELATIONSHIP BETWEEN CHARACTER AND PLOT is vital in developing your story. Often, books that ultimately fail lean too heavily on one aspect of this equation—strong characters with nothing significant to do, or a strong plot with characters no one cares about. Joining interesting, unique characters with a tightly paced plot makes for a story the reader can't put down.

As you complete the following activities, keep in mind that story should be personal. When I ask, "what's the worst thing that can happen?" I mean it specifically in the context of your characters and their world. For a shy character in a contemporary novel, exposure could be the worst possible thing; for a hero in an adventure novel, death of a mentor; for a survival story, loss of a weapon; for a romance, a betrayal of trust.

Everything is interconnected—and tying together the strands of story, plot, and world is the most difficult and the most rewarding part of writing a story that succeeds.

When looking at your overall plot, remember that opening scenes of the book often revolve around the choices a character can make. Endings typically show the changes the character's choices have resulted in. While characters are all about choices and changes, plot is about conflicts and consequences. Honing in on the way these interconnect will sharpen your storyline.

No matter what type of story you write, these elements—choices & changes, conflicts & consequences—are the driving forces of your story. In a dire epic adventure, the consequences of the hero failing may mean that the entire world ends. But that is no less important than in a romance novel, where the lovers' failure means that their personal world of happiness ends.

The skills you'll develop in this section will help you not only with writing your book, but also in revising it and in developing a pitch paragraph. Whenever you lose sight of your own story and can no longer see the forest for the trees, come back here.

CHECKLIST
for a strong opening

❑ Shows (doesn't tell) key details of the character, such as what the character lacks, what they think they need, and/or what they're afraid of

❑ Establishes some form of empathy between the main character and the reader. The reader can identify with some aspect of the character.

❑ Shows a character on the cusp of change

❑ Shows the world/setting, but only the information relevant *right then* — not the entire history of the world

❑ Shows the main character making a decision and acting upon that decision

DO NOT INCLUDE:

❑ Too much information

❑ Too many proper nouns

Example: Do use "my neighbor" instead of her name

❑ Shoe-horned description

Example: Don't use the character's mirror to describe her face

❑ Extraneous details

Example: Don't go through the steps of the alarm going off, getting dressed, boarding the bus, etc. Get to the story.

WANTS VS. NEEDS

At the beginning of your novel, what does your main character most **want**? List all that apply:

At the end of your novel, what does your main character most **need** to succeed?

THE CHANGE WORD

Your story will require your character to change in some way. After all, without change, a character is static, not dynamic, and not worthy of an entire novel. In what way must your character change and grow to succeed?

_____

_____

_____

_____

Often, the change your character must make can be summed up in one way—what emotion does the character most need in order to change? *Examples:* courage, love, faith, friendship, trust, selflessness, purpose, strength. Write it in the space below with big, strong letters—you don't want to lose sight of it!

This is your character's "Change Word,"
the word that symbolizes how they must change in order to be the hero of their own story.

CHOICES & CHANGES

In order to be active and not passive, your character must consistently make choices. Rather than let the events happen, your character must step forward and do things. Each choice should progressively show how your character changes. Consider your overall story—what series of choices leads to your character's changes? List smaller choices that your character must make, as well as the small ways those choices change them.

Example: Your main character must learn to *trust* herself and others. Her choices reflect trust. Her first choice may be to not trust a friend to help her, and the result is she failed in her task. Her character changes to attempt to trust her friend in the next situation.

Change Word:

What is it that your main character needs to find or become in order to succeed?

CHOICE	RESULT	CHANGE

THE ANTAGONIST

While characters reflect choices and changes, plot is about conflict and consequences.

What is your main character's goal for the majority of the novel? What do they want to do and/or wish would happen?

_____

_____

_____

Who or what stands in the main character's way that prevents them from being successful in their main goal?

_____

_____

_____

_____

Whatever stands in your main character's way from success is the antagonist. This is often a separate entity, and could be another person, the government, nature, etc. It could also be a concept or attitude (such as pride or prejudice). Write it in big, strong letters below so you don't lose sight of it!

This is your main character's antagonist
the person or entity that provides the problems the character must solve in order to succeed.

CONFLICT

The antagonist stands in opposition to the protagonist. They are not necessarily evil; the antagonist can simply have a different set of goals that are directly opposite of the protagonist's goals.

Protagonist's Goal	Antagonist's Goal

How do these goals conflict? How is it that only one goal can be achieved?

Note:
The antagonist may not be a person with goals; it could be a different aspect of the main character. For example, the main character is a shy girl named Amy who wants to fall in love. The protagonist is the embodiment of Brave Amy and the antagonist is Shy Amy.

CONSEQUENCES

The consequences of the protagonist's success or failure often define what the stakes of the novel are. These could be as simple as saving the world or not, or as dire as falling in love or not.

If the main character fails...	
...how will the main character's life be worse?	...how will the world as a whole be worse?

TESTING THE STORY

Often, writers don't seek feedback on their story until the story is complete. In the following spaces, distill your story. Get feedback on *just* these elements. Consider getting a new reader for this section, someone who's never read or heard of your story prior to this.

The premise of my story is that _____ needs to happen.

Initially, my main character cannot do it because:

_____
_____
_____

It's really important for her to succeed, because if she doesn't, she will be personally affected:

_____
_____
_____

Additionally, if she fails, the world as a whole will be affected because:

_____
_____
_____

Because of these stakes, she chooses to do this:

_____
_____
_____

And she's successful, because over the course of the novel, she's changed in this way:

_____
_____
_____

QUESTIONS TO ASK YOUR READER:

- Do the stakes my hero face sound important enough? Is this something worthy of her fighting to change in order to succeed?
- Would it be more logical for her to make a different decision?
- Would you root for someone who is facing these problems?
- What would make it harder for her to overcome these obstacles?
- Does this feel like a "real" problem these characters would face and care about?
- Do *you* care about this problem and its results?

Once you get feedback on these elements of your plot, you may have a better idea of what works and doesn't. Keep an eye out for stakes that aren't high enough or choices that don't really make sense for the character to take.

TIP! Use the answers to the question above not just to hone your plot, but also to develop your pitch later on, when the story is ready to be published.

OPEN & CLOSE

Often, a story arc as a whole will have a circular feel to it. While not true of every story, examine your own. Is there a way to tie the final scene with the opening scene in a way that shows how the character or the world changed? For books that are part of a series, the story may not come full circle until the last book.

How does an image in the opening parallel an image in the end of your novel?

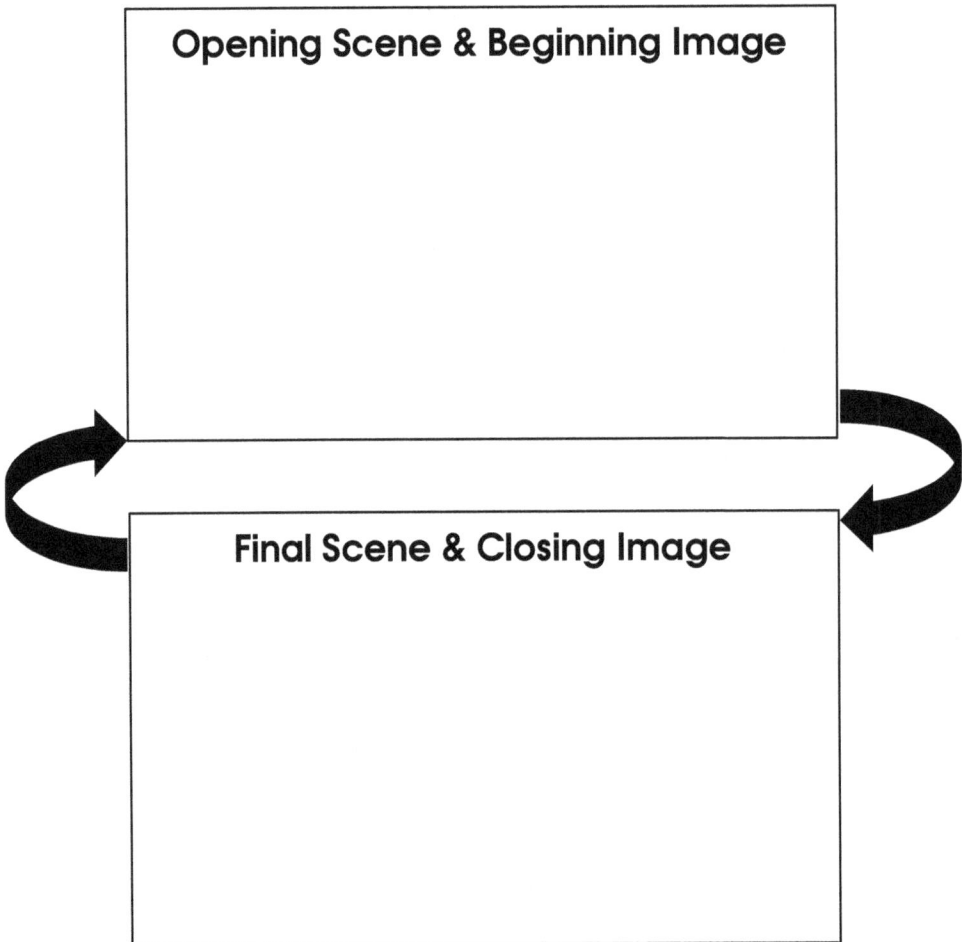

Opening Scene & Beginning Image

Final Scene & Closing Image

JOURNAL

What books have been important to you?

What book had the most impact on your life as a reader? As a writer? Why did these books resonate so deeply within you? How did those characters reflect something about yourself? How did their struggles guide your life?

_____

_____

_____

_____

_____

_____

_____

_____

_____

_____

_____

_____

_____

_____

_____

_____

_____

_____

_____

_____

_____

_____

_____

_____

_____

_____

_____

_____

END SECTION NOTES

STRUCTURE & PLOTTING

EVERY NOVEL HAS STRUCTURE, but every writer uses structure differently. Some use structure to plan their novel before they write it. Some use structure as they're writing, when they get stuck and don't know what happens next. Others use structure to revise and make sure they've touched on everything they wanted to write or to check that their pacing is tight.

However you want to use structure, make sure you use it in a way that helps you. The following activities provide a variety of structure organizing methods...and **you do not need them all.** As you learn your own process, you may find you don't need *any* of these templates and instead develop your own.

Focus on whatever helps you figure out your story. Don't get so bogged down by the format of these templates that you feel you need to do them all, and don't waste your time filling out forms instead of writing. Beware of trying to fit your book into a template where it doesn't fit. These activities are merely suggested guides to get you started; your story fits only into the mold of your making.

Extra blank pages are included in this section to get you on the right path, and extra space is throughout to help you take notes on what to change or emphasize or cut in your story as you go. Don't be intimidated—just find the story you want to tell, in the way you want to tell it.

FLOWCHART
What to do when you're stuck:

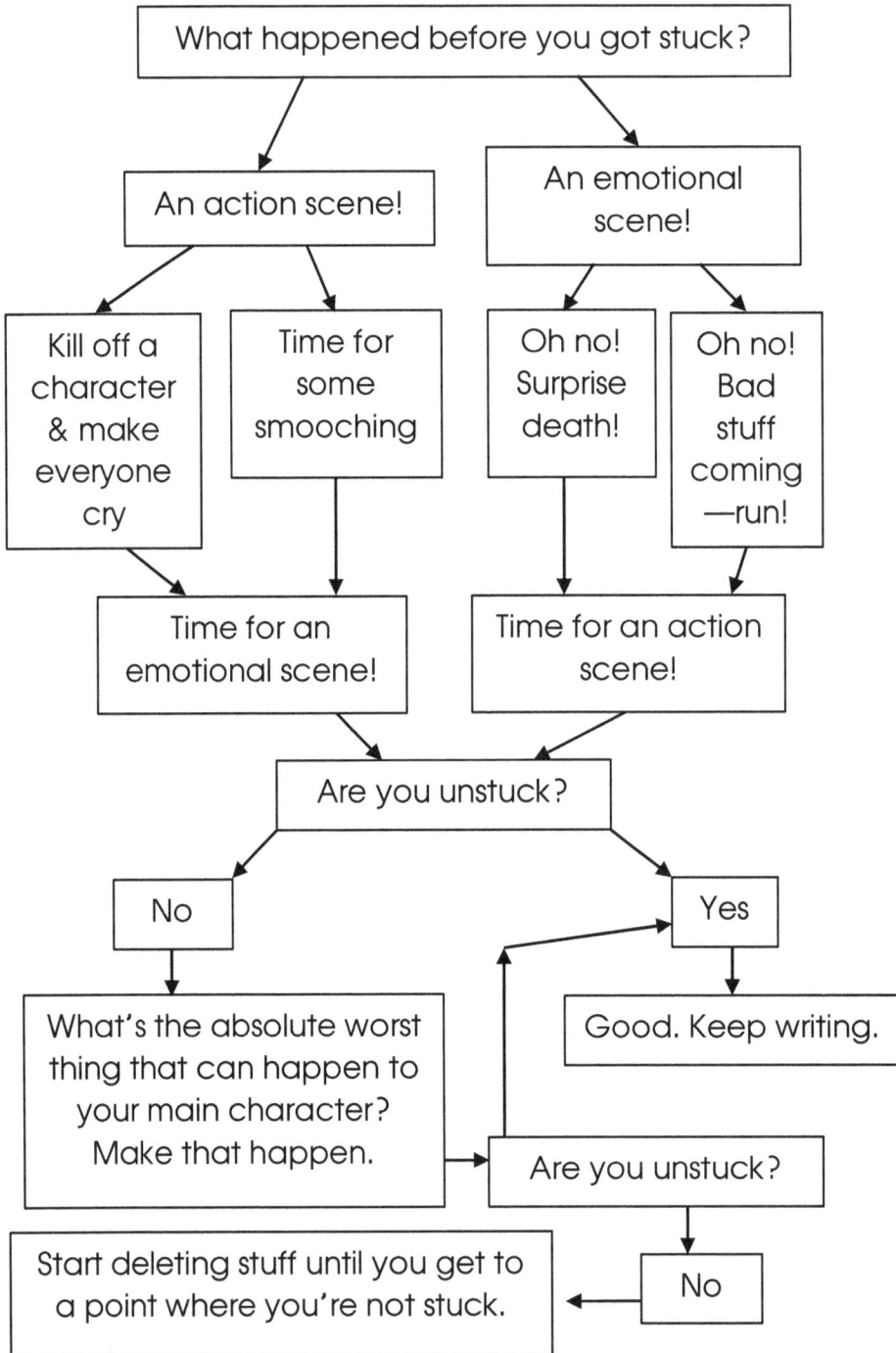

What happened before you got stuck?

An action scene!

An emotional scene!

Kill off a character & make everyone cry

Time for some smooching

Oh no! Surprise death!

Oh no! Bad stuff coming —run!

Time for an emotional scene!

Time for an action scene!

Are you unstuck?

No

Yes

What's the absolute worst thing that can happen to your main character? Make that happen.

Good. Keep writing.

Are you unstuck?

No

Start deleting stuff until you get to a point where you're not stuck.

BRAINSTORMING

Most writers don't start with the entire novel already planned out in their heads. Most have a vague idea of a handful of scenes or images, or just the beginning, or just the end, or bits and pieces. As the story develops, it often helps to think *where* the bits and pieces will go.

A common way to organize a story is in the 3-Act Structure. For more information about this, please refer to *Paper Hearts, Volume 1: Some Writing Advice.*

In the following pages, I've listed each act and then left plenty of room for you to sketch ideas, take notes on scenes to include, and organize your thoughts. Act 2 is broken in half—this act is typically longer.

I've also made a note of about how long each act should be, and how each act often ends. I find it most helpful to start with the big, momentous ends of the scenes and then fill in the blanks to everything else.

After the brainstorming pages, there are guided worksheets that go in more detail of scenes. Remember that you likely won't need everything in this section; use the activities that help you figure out your story and ignore the rest.

And finally:

ACT 1

Length:
- Roughly the first 50 pages of the average-sized novel

Scenes Typically Included:
- Opening image that establishes world and character
- A glimpse of the main character's life before the start of the story— show what's normal before you show the new normal
- Inciting incident—what kicks off the story or adventure?

End with: a scene that makes the reader *have* to keep reading to find out what happens next.

ACT 2, PART 1

Length:
- Concludes at roughly the middle of your book

Scenes Typically Included:
- The main character has a goal and works to achieve it
- Trial and error, plans and failures
- The main character grows and starts to see that the initial goal is either incorrect or harder than previously assumed
- Subplots may be introduced, or relationships complicated

End with: the mid-point of the novel; a big scene where everything changes for the main character.

ACT 2, PART 2

Length:
- From roughly the middle to just before the final scenes

Scenes Typically Included:
- Major set-backs, such as a significant loss, failure, or betrayal that the character feels keenly
- A reason to find hope regardless
- Realization that past plans won't work, but determination to continue

End with: your character has a plan of action, knows the stakes, and is facing the final trial. Courage is screwed up, the danger is known, they step forward anyway.

ACT 3

Length:
- Roughly the last 50 pages of the novel

Scenes Typically Included:
- The main character's growth over the course of the novel means he or she now has the resources to overcome the final trial

End with: a scene that promises a new world for the main character—or at least an improvement of their past world.

    If a tragedy, take away the hope and the new world.

    If a series, end with a promise that the story isn't over, or a game-changing surprise.

TURNING POINTS

Focus in on the final scenes of each of the acts, connecting the plot to the character's emotions.

Opening Scene: The beginning of the journey Show: Why does the main character decide to pursue the events of the story?	
Turning Point 1: Everything changes Show: How and why can the main character no longer go back to the way things were?	
Turning Point 2: Do or Die Show: How does the main character have to gamble everything in order to succeed?	
Closing Scene: New Beginnings Show: How has the main character earned the ending? What possibilities lie in the future?	

IN DEPTH: OPENING SCENE

Typically, the opening scenes of a novel portray the answers to the following questions:

- What does the main character lack, emotionally or physically?
- What does the main character need in order to become the hero of the story?
- What does the main character *think* he or she needs?
- What's wrong with the world of the main character?
- What outside forces drive the main character to the problems they must initially face?
- Why does the main character want to solve or ignore these problems?

Stories are not simply a list of answers. In the space below, write a scene that *shows* the answer to at least one of these questions.

_____
_____
_____
_____
_____
_____
_____
_____
_____
_____
_____
_____
_____
_____
_____
_____
_____
_____
_____

IN DEPTH: TURNING POINT 1

Typically, the scenes leading to the first turning point of a novel portray the answers to the following questions:

- What goal does the main character start with?
- How does the main character train or work toward success in the original goal?
- What failures and successes does the main character face?
- How does the original goal from the opening scene change or fall short of what needs to happen overall?
- What new goals arise?
- How does the main character feel about the successes or failures?
- How has the main character's confidence grown or shrunk?

Stories are not simply a list of answers. In the space below, write a scene that *shows* the answer to at least one of these questions.

_____
_____
_____
_____
_____
_____
_____
_____
_____
_____
_____
_____
_____
_____
_____
_____
_____
_____

IN DEPTH: TURNING POINT 2

Typically, the scenes leading to the second turning point of a novel portray the answers to the following questions:

- How are the main character's personal stakes challenged?
- How does the main character resist change?
- How does the main character feel inadequate or unable to succeed in some way?
- What has the main character lost so far? What is there still left to lose?
- How do these losses affect the main character emotionally?
- The main character must decide to risk everything to succeed—what does that entail?

Stories are not simply a list of answers. In the space below, write a scene that *shows* the answer to at least one of these questions.

_____
_____
_____
_____
_____
_____
_____
_____
_____
_____
_____
_____
_____
_____
_____
_____
_____
_____

IN DEPTH: FINAL SCENES

Typically, the final scenes of a novel portray the answers to the following questions:

- How has the main character changed from the opening of the novel to now?
- How does that change equal a resolution to the main conflict?
- How has the main character earned (or not earned) a happily ever after?
- How does the end scene show a new beginning—either a game-changing twist, or a promise of a new future for the main characters.

Stories are not simply a list of answers. In the space below, write a scene that *shows* the answer to at least one of these questions.

_____
_____
_____
_____
_____
_____
_____
_____
_____
_____
_____
_____
_____
_____
_____
_____
_____

ADDITIONAL TEMPLATES

If you are a visual person, finding a way to chart out the scenes may be beneficial to your organization. Many authors sketch ideas out on white boards, index cards, poster paper, or just plain old notebooks. These are all individual to the writer.

Following are a few different types of templates I've used over the years. I rarely do the same thing twice with each book. Each is described in much more detail in *Paper Hearts, Volume 1: Some Writing Advice.*

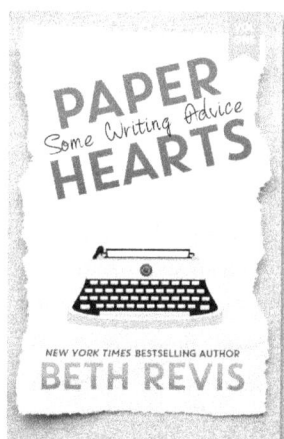

Again, it's unlikely you'll need all of these templates for one story. But it often helps me to look at the shape of a story from different angles, and if I'm stuck, breaking the story down into one of these shapes can help.

REMEMBER: Don't get bogged down with the idea of filling out all or any of the charts at the expense of just writing your story.

TIP! Watch your favorite movie and apply these templates to the story structure within them. Seeing the way other stories work with structure can help you figure out your own.

THREE HUMPS TEMPLATE

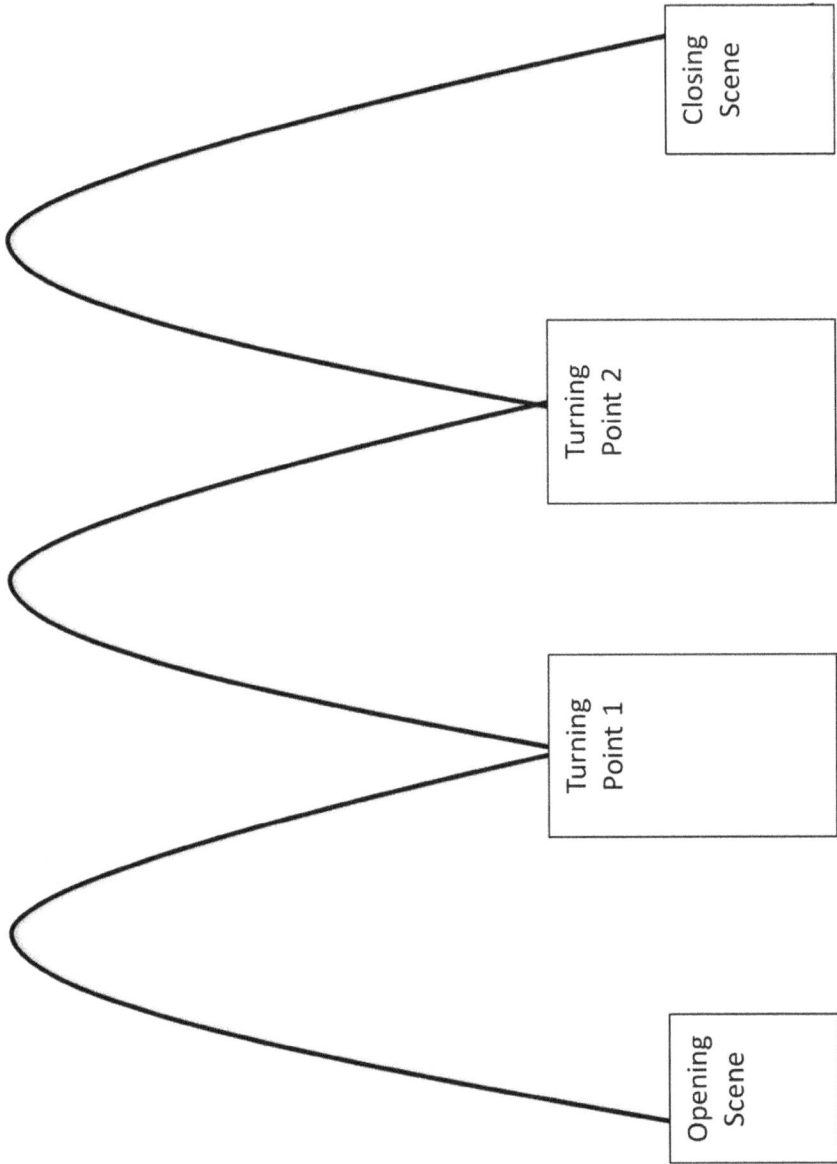

Closing Scene

Turning Point 2

Turning Point 1

Opening Scene

CHART TEMPLATE

1	2	3	4
Opening Scene			
PROBLEM: What is the Main Character (MC) like, and what's wrong with her world?	**COMPLICATIONS:** How does the MC struggle with the new changes? Who helps her? What is her relationship with the person who helps her? Romantic? Mentor?	**DANGER:** Things are getting serious. Playtime is over. The threat is very real.	**RESILIENCE:** The MC is struggling to survive, but willing to fight to the death. This part isn't about winning, it's about fighting despite the probability of failure.
Moment of Change	**Stakes Raised**	**Try & Fail**	**Final Battle**
PROCESS: What leads the MC to tackle the main problem? What is holding her back and what makes her take the plunge?	**CONFLICTS:** High action. MC is playing in the world, fighting, training, learning.	**DEATH:** There is a serious sacrifice at this point. The mentor may die, or the relationships may fall apart.	**RESOLUTION:** The MC must live with the new world. She must accept who she is now.
Main Problem	**Point of No Return**	**Darkest Moment**	*Final Scene*

CHART TEMPLATE

1	2	3	4
Opening Scene PROBLEM:	COMPLICATIONS:	DANGER:	RESILIENCE:
Moment of Change	Stakes Raised	Try & Fail	Final Battle
PROCESS:	CONFLICTS:	DEATH:	RESOLUTION:
Main Problem	Point of No Return	Darkest Moment	*Final Scene*

BARE BONES TEMPLATE

Key Scenes	Scenes in My Story
Moment of Change	
Main Problem	
Stakes Raised	
Point of No Return	
Try & Fail	
Darkest Moment	
Final Battle	
Final Scene	

EMOTIONAL TIMELINE TEMPLATE

What's Happened (External Arc)	Main Character's Emotions (Internal Arc)

SPINAL TAP CHART

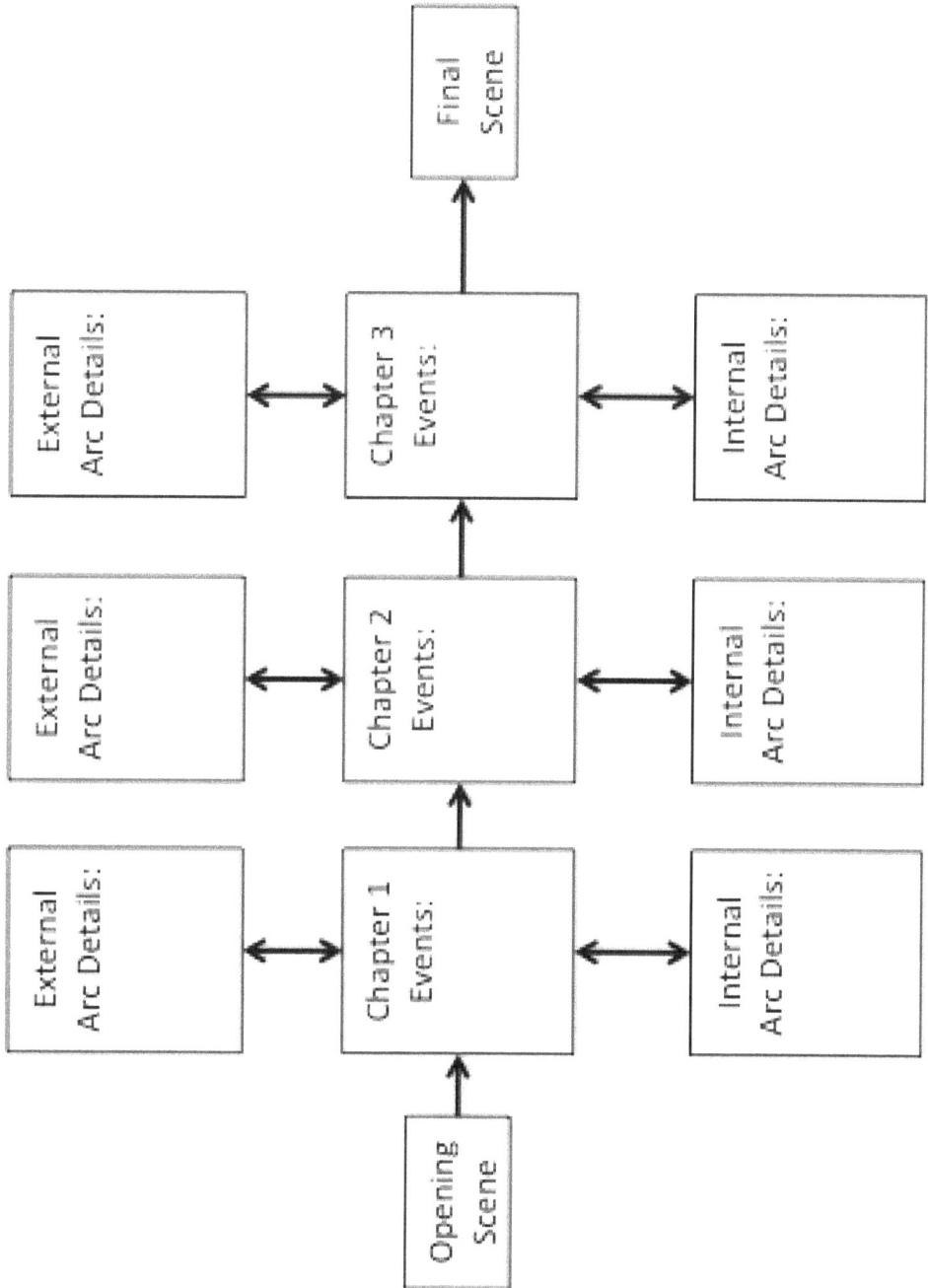

External Arc Details:	Chapter 3 Events:	Internal Arc Details:

Final Scene

External Arc Details:	Chapter 2 Events:	Internal Arc Details:

External Arc Details:	Chapter 1 Events:	Internal Arc Details:

Opening Scene

FORESHADOW

Now that you've figured out the basic structure of your plot, consider ways you can layer in clues for what will happen in your book. Foreshadowing shouldn't be so obvious it gives away the plot of your story, but should be something the reader sees by the end, upon reflection. **Remember:** You can foreshadow both physical events from the plot and emotional changes from the character.

Key Event from End Scenes:	Foreshadowed by Plot, Clue, or Object in Opening Scenes:
Key Example of Character Growth from End Scenes:	Foreshadowed by Weaker Elements of Character in Opening Scenes:

JOURNAL

What books can teach you about structure?
What's the last book you read that you could *not* put down? What made you keep turning those pages? Take a moment to analytically examine the book's structure, noting how it was put together to create an enticing read.

_____
_____
_____
_____
_____
_____
_____
_____
_____
_____
_____
_____
_____
_____
_____
_____
_____
_____
_____
_____
_____
_____
_____
_____
_____
_____
_____
_____
_____
_____

END SECTION NOTES

NEXT STEPS

YOU'VE WRITTEN AN ENTIRE BOOK. Feels good, doesn't it? Lots of people don't even make it this far. The good news is, you've already accomplished the hardest part of creating books: writing one.

Now comes the other hardest part: publishing one.

The following activities are designed to help you work with critique partners and learn the next steps you should take as you prepare to publish. Each step is important, from taking time to distance yourself from your work to learning how to both give and accept criticism.

But as you polish your novel and send it on its way, go back to the first section of this workbook. Check out your original goals and look at how far you've come. Remind yourself of your schedule for completing everything.

Be both critical of your own work and forgiving. Writing lies entirely on your shoulders, but publishing (whether self or traditional) relies on other people.

And don't forget—once this book is done, it's time to start the next one!

PUBLISHING IN 7 STEPS

Step 1: Completely finish a manuscript.

Step 2: Give it time. Gain some distance from the story, then self edit.

Step 3: Send the manuscript to readers and get feedback from them.

Step 4: Meanwhile, take time to write a pitch paragraph. Get feedback on it from new readers.

Step 4: Take time to absorb reader notes, then edit based on their feedback.

Step 5: Get feedback from new readers for manuscript & edit again (as needed).

Step 6: Once the manuscript and the pitch paragraph are perfect, decide if you would like traditional or self publication.

Traditional Publication	Self Publication
Turn pitch paragraph into query letter	Turn pitch paragraph into blurb to sell book
Submit to agents	Hire editor and complete book design before selling

Step 7: Wish for the best!

CHECKLIST
Where to find critique partners:

❑ Join writing organizations in your genre.
Examples include:
- ○ SCBWI for children's to YA writers
- ○ RWA for romance writers
- ○ SFWA for science fiction or fantasy writers

❑ Check with your local bookstore and library for local organizations, such as Writers' Coffeehouse.

❑ Reach out online to writers groups, such as:
- ○ Reddit forums specific to writing or genre
- ○ Absolute Write forum
- ○ Forum boards at writing organizations

❑ Participate in writing events, such as online contests or NaNoWriMo, and reach out to individuals you find there.

Typically, the key to finding good critique partners is to join a community of writers. Locally and online, there are groups of writers who are also seeking partners.

Before you commit to a critique partnership, run a trial. Send your pitch and a sample of a few chapters, and see if you both work well together before committing to an entire manuscript swap.

GIVING CRITIQUES

The act of giving a critique is often more valuable than getting one. Seeing the way story structure, characterization, pacing, world building and more work or don't work in a manuscript not your own helps you to develop a better eye for your work and understand what notes mean when you get them.

Please refer to *Paper Hearts, Volume 1: Some Writing* Advice for a more thorough examination. A good critique follows a typical format:

Things to include in a good critique	Things to avoid in a good critique
Instead of, or in addition to, in-line comments, compose a letter broaching the manuscript overall, focusing on the big-picture ideas of character, world, plot, pacing, etc.	Don't belabor individual lines of text. Critiques are better used as broad, big-picture analysis rather than smaller notes on individual sentences or paragraphs.
Everyone needs to know what they did well; don't ignore praise.	Don't beat a dead horse; say it once and trust the writer will understand.
If possible, phrase critiques as questions. "Why did your character do this?" is better than "Your character was dumb to do this."	Don't give suggestions of what to do; you're not writing the story.
Even if the writer is a friend, treat every aspect of the critique as professionally as possible.	Imbalanced critiques are too heavily positive or negative; strive instead to find a balance.
State upfront any biases you have, such as a preference for a type of story or genre, or if you dislike a trope, etc.	Don't focus on things irrelevant to the story. Just because you don't like something personally doesn't mean it's bad or wrong.
Create a schedule and stick to it. Communicate delays early.	Don't wait until the last minute to say you can't complete work on time.
Good critique partnerships work to help *both* writers involved.	Don't put your own career aside for someone else's.

CHECKLIST FOR CRITIQUES
Make sure your critique examines these points:

❑ Characters
- o Did the main character feel real?
- o Did the side characters feel real?
- o Does the story reflect diversity?
- o Does the characters' motivations feel real?
- o Are those motivations clear and understandable?
- o Did the character have personal stakes in the story that were clear?
- o Did the way the characters interact feel true?
- o Are there too many or too few characters?

❑ Plot
- o Is there a balance between action scenes and emotional scenes?
- o Does the action rise steadily?
- o Does the story progress naturally?
- o Is there a reasonable balance between actions and reactions from your characters?

❑ World
- o Does the world feel real?
- o Does the author use all senses—sight, sound, touch, taste, feel—to describe key aspects of the setting?
- o Is the setting either vividly real (if part of the story) or unobtrusively presented (if not)?
- o Does the world accurately reflect a realistic world, including diverse background characters, economies, beliefs, etc.
- o Does the world work for the genre? I.e. historical world with no anachronisms.

❑ Logic
- o Did the characters act logically, given the situations at hand?
- o Were there smarter or simpler solutions they should have attempted first?
- o Are explanations of alien ideas (i.e. a speculative fiction angle, a difficult medical procedure) presented simply and unobtrusively?
- o Do any fictional rules—such as a magic system—follow a logical set of in-world rules?
- o Are things too easy for your characters?

❑ Pacing
- o Any parts feel too slow?
- o Any parts feel confusing because the story is moving too quickly?
- o Do characters seem passive by not making choices?
- o Do characters seem erratic by acting too quickly?

❑ Prose
- o On a craft level, is the writing solid?
- o Are action scenes written with an eye toward faster reading (more white space, shorter and punchier sentences)?
- o Are there any particularly beautiful turns of phrases?
- o Is there purple prose or overwritten areas?

❑ Overall notes
- o What parts of the book were your favorite?
- o What themes did you identify within the text?
- o What parts of the book needed more work?

TIPS FOR DEVELOPING A PITCH PARAGRAPH

A pitch paragraph is used throughout your writing career, regardless of path. Learning the style of pitch paragraphs is important; you will use it to write queries or sell your book.

Before you write your own pitch paragraph, read as many as you can. There are slight style differences between pitch paragraphs used in query letters and those used as blurbs to sell books, so focus on reading examples from ones that match your goal.

TIPS

- Focus on the main plotline only.
- Whenever possible, don't use proper nouns.
    - Example: use a relationships (aunt) instead of a name (Aunt May) or a location (capital city) instead of an unknown fantasy world name
- Focus on both the world stakes and personal stakes of the main character.
- Clearly show what the conflict or problem to be solved is, with obvious consequences should the main character fail.
- Inject some tone of the novel into the pitch, but err on the side of clarity.
- You don't need to explicitly state the end of the novel, but make it clear what the end is about.
    - Example: if your query ends with "Amy must uncover who the murderer is," then the reader knows the end of the book is about solving the mystery without knowing who the murderer is.
- Write in 3rd person point of view and present tense, regardless of the view/tense the book is written in.
- Remember: it doesn't have to be specifically one paragraph. Break it up for stylistic purposes as needed.
    - It should still only be about 200 words long.
- **Go back to the early sections of this workbook and review how you simplified your story for yourself.**

THE OTHER PITCH

It's often easier to write someone else's pitch than your own. Use the space below to distill your story into the following key elements, then ask a partner to write your pitch for you. Meanwhile, you write their pitch based on the elements they discussed. Go over the results together, comparing where the simplification enhanced the query or where you need to add more detail to make the real meaning of your story come across.

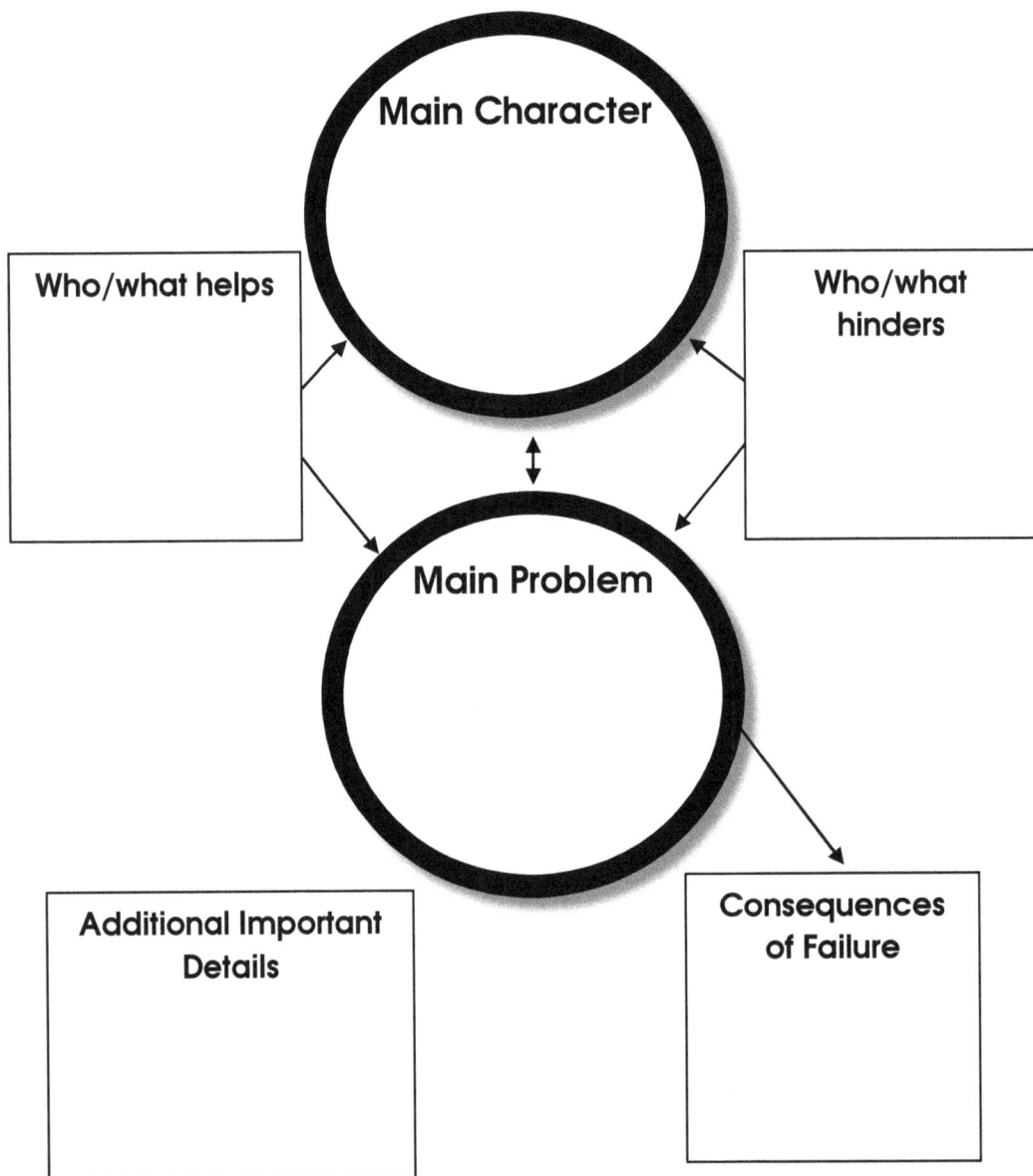

Main Character

Who/what helps

Who/what hinders

Main Problem

Additional Important Details

Consequences of Failure

PITCH PARAGRAPH BLANKS

Below are some sample blanks to fill in your pitch paragraph. *Do not just copy and paste the results into your pitch paragraph*: these are generic, and simply to be used to determine the important information for your pitch and show you how the query can be rather simple.

THE HERO'S QUEST PITCH:
1. Adjective about main character (such as age)
2. Main character's name
3. Location at start of story
4. Feelings of dissatisfaction or happiness with current status
5. Why character is happy or not
6. Inciting incident of story
7. Task or quest to complete
8. Personal stakes
9. World stakes

(1) _____(2) _____ currently lives in

(3)_____ and feels (4) _____

because (5)_____.

However, when (6)_____,

everything changes. Now she must (7)_____

_____.

If she fails, she will personally lose (8) _____

_____

and her world will be worse off because (9)_____

_____.

THE DUAL NARRATIVE PITCH:

1. Adjective for character, such as age
2. First character's name
3. Current location or situation the first character deals with at the start of the novel.
4. Inciting incident for first character
5. First character's goals or personal stakes
6. Second character's name
7. Second character's status, location, or situation
8. Second character's goals or stakes.
9. Circumstances of meeting, or how things change when they meet.
10. New goal they both most work towards
11. Stakes and consequences of if they fail.

(1) _____(2) _____ currently

(3)_____. She

decides to (4) _____

because (5) _____.

(6) _____ is (7) _____.

He currently (8) _____.

When they meet, (9) _____.

Now they must work together to (10) _____.

If they fail, (11) _____.

THE WANTS VS. NEEDS PITCH:
1. Adjective for character, such as age
2. Main character's name
3. Main character's original desire
4. Inciting incident
5. Character growth
6. Personal stakes
7. Twist
8. New goal
9. Worst possible outcome for your main character

(1) _____(2) _____ currently wants

nothing more than (3)_____. But

when she is faced with (4) _____,

she must learn to (5) _____.

Failing to do this means (6)_____.

But what she doesn't know is (7) _____.

Now she must (8) _____,

because if she can't, then (9)_____.

TIPS FOR DEVELOPING A QUERY LETTER

ELEMENTS OF A QUERY LETTER:
- Pitch Paragraph
- Statistics Paragraph
- Biography Paragraph

STATISTICS PARAGRAPH:

- Short, to the point, and just the facts
- This paragraph either opens the letter or follows the pitch paragraph.
- Must include the following information:
  - Title of book
  - Genre
  - Word count (round up to the nearest thousand)
  - Age range, if writing anything other than adult
- Can include:
  - Whether the book is a stand-alone, first of a series, or is a stand-alone with series potential
  - Target audience and/or "comp titles"
- Comp titles are similar books already on the market. When comparing your book to other books:
  - Don't include the most popular books in your genre (i.e. *Twilight* or Harry Potter). You want to show you deeply know and understand your genre, not that you're only aware of the heavy-hitters.
  - Match genre, style, and voice to your work; *don't* make it a stretch (i.e. "My book has the fast pace of this totally different book and the romance of this book that has nothing to do with either of these titles!")
  - Comp titles should be immediately apparent how they work with your book.
  - A popular way to phrase comp titles include:
    - "My book is X meets Y."
    - "Fans of Book A will enjoy this element of my book."
    - "My book is Book B, but with a twist."
  - When in doubt, don't use a comp title.

BIOGRAPHY PARAGRAPH:

- Usually just a sentence or two long.
- Only mention relevant publishing credentials
    - Include if you've published novels before
    - Include publications in respected presses, such as magazines or journals relevant to your topic
    - Do not include every publication just because you were published—school journals or technical manuals are not relevant
- Include any professional writing organization you're a member of
- Education and careers only matter if they are relevant to your story
    - MFAs in writing, or a degree in your novel's subject matter
    - For writers of children's to teen books, experience working with children or teens is relevant
- Can include a social media presence, but limit to only the top 2-3 links and only mention follow counts if they're significant.
    - Celebrity authors or authors with significant platforms (i.e. over a million followers) may use their following as marketing
    - Without a significant following, agents will still want to see your social media presence to know if you understand the platforms and use them responsibly.
- Write this paragraph in first person point of view (i.e. you own voice), not third.
- Do *not* be worried if you have no writing credentials. Debut authors are not expected to start with careers already established. This paragraph can be as simple as "My name is X and I currently live in Y."
- Conclude by thanking the agent for reading, but:
    - Do not grovel that she read your book
    - Do not say she'll regret not signing you
    - Do not belittle yourself
    - Do not belittle other writers
    - Seriously, just say "Thank you for reading" and sign off

PERSONALIZING THE QUERY:

- Much is made about how queries should be personalized to an agent. Using the agent's name in the salutation—rather than "Dear Agent" or "Dear Sir"—is enough.
- *If* you have a referral or a direct comp title, mention that.

SAMPLE QUERY LETTER

Dear Ms. Heifetz,

Seventeen-year-old Amy has no desire to become one of the first colonists on a new planet--but her parents do. So she agrees to be cryogenically frozen for the journey, even if it means giving up the life she loves on Earth.

Much later, Elder--part of the generations of workers born on the ship-- begins his training as the future commander. He has no idea of the cargo of cryogenically frozen people hidden beneath his feet.

Then Amy wakes up fifty years early.

Amy must now adjust to life without her still-frozen parents on board a space ship that is vastly different from her home on Earth. Trapped by both the metal walls of the ship and the lies that keep it running, Amy discovers her cryo chamber hadn't malfunctioned--someone had tried to kill her. As more and more helplessly frozen victims are unplugged, Amy combines her knowledge of the past with Elder's knowledge of the ship to find and stop the murderer...before Amy's parents are the next victims.

Complete at 80,000 words, ACROSS THE UNIVERSE is science fiction for teens who don't like science fiction. The character-driven plot with a focus on mystery, secrets, and an unreliable narrator will appeal to fans of Mary Pearson's THE ADORATION OF JENNA FOX.

I am currently a high school world literature teacher and an active member of SCBWI, having been published in and working as the copy editor of the state SCBWI magazine. Additionally, I run a blog on writing for MG and YA audiences. I can be found online at bethrevis.com.

I am prepared to submit the entire manuscript upon your request. Thank you for your time and consideration with this project. Below are the first five pages as a sample of my writing.

Sincerely,
Beth Revis
bethrevis@gmail.com
bethrevis.com

Dear [Agent name],

[Pitch paragraph]:_____

_____

_____

_____

_____

_____

_____

_____

_____

_____

[Title]_____ is a [genre] _____

complete at [word count]_____ words. It would appeal to fans of

_____

_____

[Biography]_____

_____

_____

CHECKLIST

After you've finished your manuscript and sent it out, what do you do next?

❑ Write the next book

JOURNAL

What are you most proud of?

Now that you've completed an entire novel, what part of the process or finished product are you proudest of? What parts were the most joyful for you to write? Most painful? Most worthwhile?

_____
_____
_____
_____
_____
_____
_____
_____
_____
_____
_____
_____
_____
_____
_____
_____
_____
_____
_____
_____
_____
_____
_____
_____
_____
_____
_____
_____

END SECTION NOTES

ABOUT THE AUTHOR

Beth Revis is the author of the *New York Times* bestselling novel *Across the Universe* and its sequels, as well as *The Body Electric, A World Without You, Star Wars: Rebel Rising,* more than a dozen published short stories, and the nonfiction Paper Hearts series. She currently lives in rural North Carolina with her boys: one husband, one son, and two massive dogs.

Prior to becoming a full time novelist, Beth spent a lot of time writing books that didn't sell. *Paper Hearts* is her way of giving back to the community of writers who aided her.

Would you like Beth to speak to your writer's group or classroom? Please contact her at authorbethrevis@gmail.com for rates and availability.

Find Beth online at bethrevis.com. Sign up for her newsletter at http://bit.ly/bethnews and never miss a new release.

 @bethrevis

 @bethrevis

 @authorbethrevis

PRAISE FOR BETH'S BOOKS

ACROSS THE UNIVERSE

"Who Should Read This: Well, sci-fi and mystery fans will love it, but so will any girl or boy who's ever sat in a room full of quiet conformists and wanted to scream at them all, 'Wake up!'" —MTV.com

A MILLION SUNS

"Setting and plot are the heart and soul of this ripping space thriller, and they're unforgettable." —*Kirkus*, starred review

SHADES OF EARTH

"[Revis has a gift] as a propulsive storyteller with a knack for jarring surprises and raising the stakes." —*Booklist*

THE BODY ELECTRIC

"Short chapters...make for addictive reading, and the reverie-within-reverie sequences are vibrantly rendered games of cat and mouse. ...Revis gives a masterly blend of worlds familiar and new in this standalone SF mystery." —*Publisher's Weekly*

A WORLD WITHOUT YOU

"Revis's account of grief, loss, first love, and anguish, presented through a lens of mental illness, is a must-read." —*Voya*, starred review

COMPLETE YOUR COLLECTION

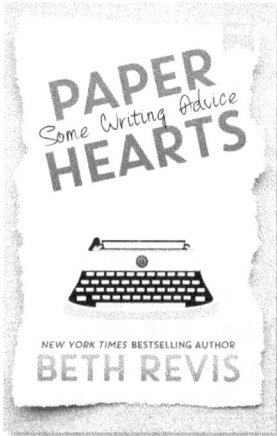

The book that started it all, covering the basics of writing from idea to revision, with practical advice born from more than a decade of writing more than 200 million words of fiction. Includes charts on story structure, an appendix with common writing problems and possible solutions, and much, much more.

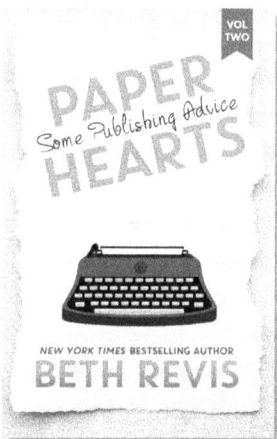

When you're ready to take your book to the next stage, PAPER HEARTS VOLUME 2 serves as a guide. With unbiased information on multiple possible publishing paths, this book provides practical resources to determine whether your book should be traditionally or self published and gives specific examples on successful practices for both paths. Go from query to interviewing agents to working with traditional publishing editors, as well as avoiding pitfalls in self publishing, developing a book, and distributing it across markets.

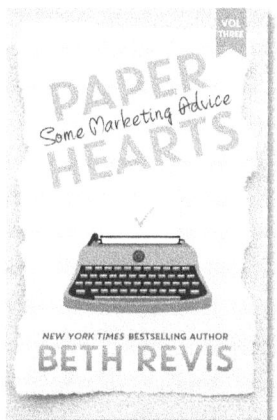

Designed with new writers in mind, Volume 3 focuses on tried-and-true practices for writers to help get their books in front of audiences. Including specific information on what's worthwhile and what's a waste of time and money, this volume will help give a foundation for ways for authors to enhance their career goals.

www.ingramcontent.com/pod-product-compliance
Lightning Source LLC
Chambersburg PA
CBHW081648270326
41933CB00018B/3384